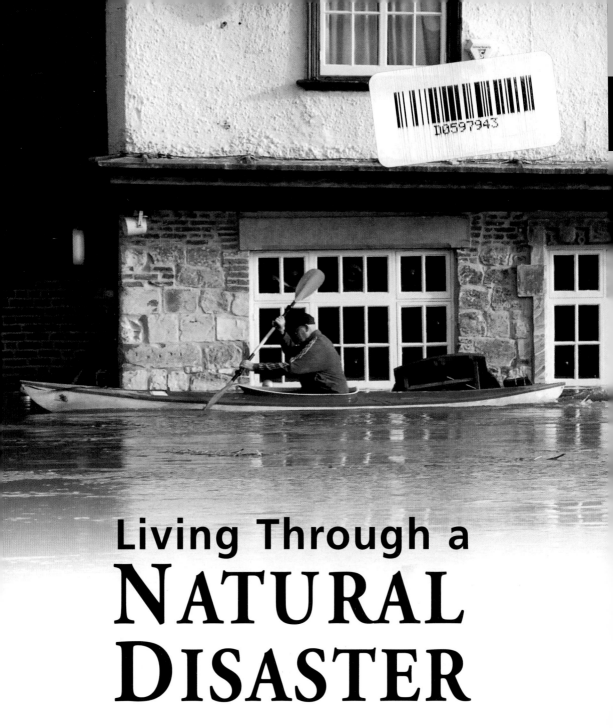

Living Through a
NATURAL DISASTER

By Eve Recht

CELEBRATION PRESS
Pearson Learning Group

The following people from **Pearson Learning Group**
have contributed to the development of this product:

Joan Mazzeo, Dorothea Fox **Design** | **Editorial** Leslie Feierstone Barna, Cindy Kane

Christine Fleming **Marketing** | **Publishing Operations** Jennifer Van Der Heide

Production Laura Benford-Sullivan

Content Area Consultants Dr. Amy Rabb-Liu and Dr. Charles Liu

The following people from **DK** have
contributed to the development of this product:

Art Director Rachael Foster

Martin Wilson **Managing Art Editor** | **Managing Editor** Marie Greenwood

Kath Northam **Design** | **Editorial** Hannah Wilson

Cynthia Frazer **Picture Research** | **Production** Gordana Simakovic

Richard Czapnik, Andy Smith **Cover Design** | **DTP** David McDonald

Consultant Keith Lye

Dorling Kindersley would like to thank: Northern Territory Library and Information Services, Australia, for Cyclone Tracy witness accounts; David Ferguson for additional consultancy; Rose Horridge in the DK Picture Library; Ed Merrit for cartography; and Johnny Pau for additional cover design work.

Photographs: Every effort has been made to secure permission and provide appropriate credit for photographic material. The publisher deeply regrets any omission and pledges to correct errors called to its attention in subsequent editions.

Unless otherwise acknowledged, all photographs are the property of Dorling Kindersley.

Photo locators denoted as follows: Top (T), Center (C), Bottom (B), Left (L), Right (R), Background (Bkgd)

Picture Credits: 001 Ronald Hudson/Fotolia; **003** Evgeny Dubinchuk/Fotolia; **004** OAR/ERL/National Severe Storms Laboratory (NSSL)/NOAA; **005B** ESTEBAN FELIX/AP Images; **005C** AP Images; **005T** Bettmann/Corbis; **006B** Bettmann/Corbis; **007** Photobank.kiev.ua/Fotolia; **007BKGD** B747/Fotolia; **009** FLPA; **010BR** AP Images; **010L** Bettmann/Corbis; **010TR** AP Images; **011** AP Images; **012B** David Wall/Alamy; **012T** Robert Kyllo/Shutterstock; **013** Mary Evans Picture Library/Alamy; **014** Julia Waterlow/Eye Ubiquitous/Alamy; **016** Christiane Alt-Eppin/Fotolia; **017B** STR New/Reuters; **017T** Dewater/Fotolia; **018** FRANCOIS TOURON/AP Images; **019L** INTERFOTO/History/Alamy; **019R** AP Images; **020** Keren Su/China Span/Alamy; **021** ESTEBAN FELIX/AP Images; **022B** Ivalin/Shutterstock; **022T** JAIRO CAJINA/AFP/Newscom; **023** Scott Dalton/AP Images; **024B** JPL/NASA; **024T** Lisa F. Young/Fotolia; **025** ORLANDO SIERRA/AFP/Newscom; **026** ekulik2011/Fotolia; **027** Daniel Aguilar/REUTERS; **027B** Heeb Christian/Prisma Bildagentur AG/Alamy; **028** William Berry/Fotolia; **029B** YOAV LEMMER/AFP/Newscom; **029C** Library of Congress Prints and Photographs Division Washington; **029T** ABIR ABDULLAH/EPA/Newscom; **030L** Rafiquar Rahman/Reuters; **030R** ORLANDO SIERRA/AFP/Getty Images/Newscom; **032** B747/Fotolia

All other images: ᴅᴋ Dorling Kindersley © 2005. For further information see www.dkimages.com

ISBN: 0-7652-5244-9

Color reproduction by Colourscan, Singapore
Printed in Mexico
33   20

1-800-321-3106
www.pearsonlearning.com

Contents

Extreme Weather   4

The Story of Cyclone Tracy   6

The Huang He Flood   13

El Niño Brings Drought   21

Handling Natural Disasters   29

Index   32

Extreme Weather

Weather, predictable or not, is always with us.
For most of us, the weather is more or less unsurprising—
colder in winter and warmer in summer. There are rainy
days or clear skies, and the occasional thunderstorm or
early snowfall. Sometimes, though, weather can be
much harsher than normal. Some places in the world
may experience gale-force winds, whereas other places
might have heavy rain for weeks. Still other places
might have no rain for long periods of time.

Extreme weather can be very dangerous, but
when it is predicted, people can make preparations
to lessen its damage. However, it is not always possible
to know ahead of time that bad weather is on its way.
For example, tornadoes like the one shown on this page
can form very quickly and can be very destructive.
When such violent weather arrives unexpectedly,
the toll in human life may be high because people
do not have time to seek shelter or to evacuate.

A tropical cyclone almost destroyed an Australian city in 1974.

Severe floods brought death and hardship to many thousands of Chinese in 1933.

Drought brought disaster to several Central American countries in 1997 and 1998.

Tropical cyclones are among the most extreme storms people experience. These storms develop and build over the oceans in the tropics, close to the equator. If they strike a coastline, they may cause a great deal of damage. In this book, you can read about Tracy, a small but severe cyclone that hit the city of Darwin, Australia, in late 1974. It became the worst natural disaster that any Australian city had ever experienced.

Many people who live beside rivers worry about extreme rainfall. Too much rain can cause water levels to rise and spill over the riverbanks, flooding farmland and homes. Along China's rivers, floods are most common in the summer, when seasonal winds bring rain clouds over the land from the ocean. You can read about the disastrous results produced when the Huang He, a river in China, flooded in 1933.

Drought can be just as extreme as cyclones and floods. In a drought, rain may not fall in a region for months or years. As plants and animals die from lack of water, many people face economic hardship and starvation. In this book, you can read about a severe drought that began in Central America in 1997 and find out how different countries, including Costa Rica, handled the disaster.

The Story of Cyclone Tracy

On December 24, 1974, the residents of Darwin, Australia, were enjoying the summer. It was Christmas Eve, and many people were celebrating. At about 9:30 P.M., the weather service began broadcasting cyclone warnings. Most people were too busy preparing for Christmas Day to pay much attention to the warnings. Then, just after midnight, the cyclone hit Darwin with heavy rain and winds of more than 125 miles per hour.

By the next morning, Darwin had been devastated. Most buildings were flattened, and there was no power. Trucks and planes had been blown around like toys. During Cyclone Tracy's night of destruction in Darwin, more than sixty people were killed, and hundreds had been injured.

The cyclone, officially named Tracy, left the city of Darwin in ruins.

What Is a Cyclone?

Tropical cyclones are powerful storm systems that develop over warm ocean waters. In North America, these storms are called hurricanes, whereas in Australia they are called cyclones. In eastern Asia, they are known as typhoons. A tropical cyclone develops when warm, moist air is sucked into an area of low pressure. Over time, huge thunderclouds build up and strong winds begin to rotate around the storm center.

A Night of Destruction

Like many other Darwin residents, Bob Collins didn't pay too much attention to the cyclone warnings on December 24. In the evening, he was at his home just outside the city. Bob described the dramatic events of the night that followed in this way:

// At about midnight, it was clear that this was going to be something significant and scary. The wind just kept on getting stronger and stronger. It went past the point where you'd ever experienced anything like it before.... **//**

// And then, in the early hours of the morning ... there was this enormous sort of ripping, tearing sound and in a matter of seconds, the entire roof just peeled off the house.... It sucked the ceilings out.... And we were just surrounded by the brick walls of the house, with rain and wind just shooting into the house. It was absolutely terrifying. **//**

Bob Collins and his friends drove to his office building, which was "cyclone-proof." A cyclone-proof building is usually constructed with steel and concrete. Bob described the difficult trip to his office:

> ❚❚ The three of us jammed ourselves into this four-wheel drive and took off ... in the eye of the storm. There was of course this artificial lull. And the sight that I saw in the headlights of the vehicle ... was just extraordinary. Trees laying ... across the road.... [Then,] the storm had actually come back the other way.... We were very lucky to make it. ❚❚

The "Eye"

The area of calm in the middle of a cyclone is called the eye. It is surrounded by a wall of thick clouds, driving rains, and spiraling winds. When the eye of the storm is directly overhead, the winds suddenly drop and the sky clears for a short time (usually an hour or two). After the eye has passed, the fierce winds and rain start again, but this time they blow from the opposite direction.

layers of
spiraling winds

eye

wall

Cyclone cross-section

Not many of Darwin's residents ventured out into the cyclone. Rob Wesley-Smith stayed in his apartment. He told the story of his struggle to save his photographs and personal papers in this way:

> ❚❚ The suction ... was just unbelievable. I couldn't stop things blowing out. I tried to shut the door ... but the building must have been moving and the thing just swung open.... I'd gone to bed ... and woke up with a cyclone raging. ❚❚

A Morning of Devastation

On the morning of December 25, the residents of Darwin emerged from their safe places to face the destruction of their city. What they saw was shocking. Some people described the scene as looking like a battlefield. Others said the city had been turned into a huge garbage dump.

That morning, Bob Collins drove to the ambulance station to see if he could help anyone. He described the scene around the city:

> **** Seeing those big, high-tension power lines, the actual steel poles that held them up, twisted like licorice.... I went past the old Darwin airport.... Millions of dollars worth, literally, of aircraft had just been blown up in a heap like ... garbage....**//**

Coping With the Chaos

The police began cleaning up early in the morning. Service people from the army, navy, and air force joined them on December 26. They brought along specialized equipment, such as electricity generators, to help restore utilities. Doctors and nurses arrived to treat people who were injured or in shock. They brought basic supplies, such as food, blankets, and tents that would provide temporary shelter for those who had been left homeless.

Bob Collins, one of many ordinary residents who volunteered to help, described how the streets were cleared:

// Graders and bulldozers [were] out on the roads, and they'd actually graded tracks through the debris, and moved bits of houses and sheet iron and broken glass that was everywhere. **//**

The photos below show the remains of a row of stilt houses.

This photo shows aircraft that were picked up by the winds and dropped upside down.

Thousands of people had lost nearly everything they owned. Houses were destroyed and their contents blown away or soaked with rain and mud. It was difficult to look for things in the mess of rubble, uprooted trees, and mangled cars. The city was in ruins, and the government's emergency team decided to evacuate everyone as soon as possible.

Darwin's population when Tracy hit was about 44,000. By December 31, only about 11,000 people remained. About 26,000 people left by air and more than 7,000 by road. Many people did not return to Darwin for several years. Others never returned.

Dawn Lawrie described the strange evacuation scene:

// The evacuation was a once in a lifetime experience.... It was a mass evacuation ... [but] there was quite a stillness and a quietness. I worked assisting them [the people] to get to the plane.... We crammed the people on. I think we hold the world record for getting numbers of actual people in the aircraft. //

Darwin Today

During the next thirty years, Darwin was rebuilt. Strict regulations were introduced to ensure that all new buildings could withstand the force of a cyclone. Some buildings were built to allow winds to blow through them, leaving the main structure standing. Others used reinforcing steel rods to fix them firmly to the ground. Public cyclone shelters were also built.

Cyclones are most likely to occur during the wet season, which runs from October to March. During this period, the people of Darwin are on their guard. Hopefully, they will be better prepared should another disastrous visitor like Cyclone Tracy arrive.

All new buildings erected in Darwin—even those delivered by truck—are cyclone-proof.

Today, Darwin has been rebuilt and is an active city again.

The Huang He Flood

The Huang He winds its way down from the mountainous region in the heart of China. The river then meanders eastward across the vast North China Plain before emptying into the Yellow Sea.

The lower section of the river often floods the flat plains, making that region a dangerous place to live. However, the flooding brings riches as well as disaster. The floods leave behind a layer of silt, making the plains fertile. The crops grown there feed millions of people.

In 1933, the Huang He proved once again that it was a danger that could not be ignored. It unleashed a terrible flood that swept through towns, villages, and farmland. It killed thousands of people and left millions homeless.

ASIA

Huang He

Beijing

Huang He

North China Plain

Yellow Sea

Chang Jiang

China

Shanghai

PAC OC

Southeast Asia

N
W · E
S

The flood forced people to flee by boat.

What Is a Flood?

There are two basic types of river flood. A regular flood happens when the water level slowly rises, then overflows its banks. A more dangerous flash flood happens when a great amount of rain falls in a short time, causing a wall of water to suddenly rush over an area.

Human activity can cause floods. Soil and vegetation absorb rain. When trees are cut down and the land is covered with buildings and roads, rain cannot be absorbed into the soil. Instead, it runs off into ditches and storm sewers. If there is heavy rain, water can overflow these places, causing a flood.

The Yellow River

Huang He means "yellow river" in Chinese. The river takes its name from the tons of yellow-colored silt that it collects on its journey through the river gorges before it reaches the plains. It is this silt that is so fertile and that nourishes the surrounding land when the river floods.

The silt settles on the riverbed, and as it builds up, the level of the water is raised. In times of heavy rain, the river overflows its banks, flooding the region.

For hundreds of years, the people who lived along the Huang He tried to find ways to control the frequent river floods. They dug out the silt and built canals to direct the water elsewhere. However, the silt continued to cause the level of the riverbed to rise. Over the years, the higher riverbed raised the level of the water in the river. In some places, the water flowed along a riverbed of mud that was more than 15 feet above the level of the surrounding plains.

The people finally decided that the best way to stop the river from overflowing was to build up the banks of the river, forming high walls called dikes. As the diagram on the next page shows, this action only made a dangerous situation even worse.

This is the muddy, yellow Huang He today. At about 3,000 miles long, it is one of the world's longest rivers. Much of the Huang He flows across a very flat region, changing its course from time to time.

Heavy Rain

The rainy season **in** central China occurs every June and July. In June 1933, the farmers strengthened the dikes as they did each year. However, the **rains** in July were so heavy **that** the water overflowed the dikes in some places. People worked as fast as they could to build the dikes higher.

How the Huang He Became So High

silt piles up on riverbed

river overflows its banks

1 Silt collected on the riverbed, pushing up the water level. During heavy rain, the water spilled over the banks.

dike

river contained within dikes

2 Farmers built dikes along the riverbanks. The dikes usually stopped the water from flowing out onto surrounding fields.

water level rises

dike raised

silt builds up

3 As more silt built up, the water kept rising. Farmers built the dikes higher, and the water level became dangerously high.

As the weeks passed, the rains kept falling, and the river level continued to rise. A huge amount of water now flowed along its high riverbed above the farmland, villages, and towns on the plains.

The swiftly moving water pounded the walls of the dikes until they could no longer withstand the force. The dikes began to break. People frantically tried to repair the gaps, plugging them with bundles of kaoliang stalks, rocks, and earth. The rushing water kept pulling away more and more material from the dikes, making the gaps even wider.

Today, the dikes along many of China's rivers are reinforced with a crisscross of steel pipes.

Kaoliang

In the past, dikes were made mainly of bundles of kaoliang stalks, a grain that grows on the North China Plain. Kaoliang, which is also called Chinese sorghum, has been an important building material and food crop in China for thousands of years. Its seeds, or grain, are used for animal feed.

maize   kaoliang

Chinese crops

The Huang He Overflows

Under increasing pressure, many of the river dikes collapsed without warning. Water rushed through more than 1,000 breaks, some a mile wide. The entire river emptied onto the plains, creating a huge flood of muddy, swirling water.

People fled for their lives, but thousands drowned in the massive waterfalls that poured down from the high banks of the river. Some people survived by climbing trees and rooftops. They waited in these high places, enduring hunger, thirst, and the pouring rain, hoping to be rescued.

Other people fled by boat. They gathered whatever possessions they could and desperately paddled away from the flooded areas. As they escaped, they tried to rescue anyone who was stranded.

Waters of the Huang He flooded about 4,500 square miles of farmland, villages, and towns.

In the towns, streets became rivers along which people fled in flat-bottomed boats called sampans.

After the floodwaters retreated, homes that were not washed away were buried under a thick covering of mud. More than three million people were left homeless and had to dig in the mud to find scraps of material to rebuild their houses. The crops on the plains had also been ruined, bringing starvation and famine to thousands.

The Huang He Today

To prepare for future floods, trees and other vegetation were planted along the river. Plants help to absorb rainfall and to reduce soil erosion that washes silt into the river.

However, many people who live along the Huang He are faced with a different problem today. After decades of drought, deforestation, and mismanagement, some parts of the Huang He are nearly dry. Since local people, farms, and industries rely on the river for their water supply, this situation is causing huge problems. Du Paiyuan is the manager of a copper factory in the city of Taiyun. He explained how the lack of water was affecting his workers:

> **** Some of our employees have had no water for days. They can't clean their homes.... They can only take showers once a week. **//**

To deal with the low water levels, the government has begun to dig wells and provide money for better irrigation systems. It has considered building canals to bring water to the Huang He from the Chang Jiang (Yangtze River). However, this project would be very expensive and may not provide the needed amount of water.

Today, some parts of the Huang He are almost dry.

El Niño Brings Drought

The people of Central America know that El Niño is a force to be reckoned with. El Niño is a pattern of winds and ocean currents that affects Earth's weather. In different parts of the world at the same time, it can trigger storms, floods, or drought, which is an unusually long period of extremely dry weather.

In 1997 and 1998, El Niño produced a terrible drought in much of Central America. Crops and farm animals died, and forest fires raged across the parched land. Food and water shortages affected almost 1 million people.

This Guatemalan farmer's crops were destroyed by El Niño-related drought.

An Unstable Environment

The countries of Central America contain a diverse range of plants and animals. The region is home to tropical rain forests, swamps, beaches, and mountains. It is an important agricultural area, and many of its residents make a living producing coffee, sugar, and maize.

In October 1998, soon after the drought ended, Hurricane Mitch brought floods to Honduras and to Nicaragua (above).

Unfortunately, the rich and varied environment of the region has suffered over the years. It lies in an unstable part of Earth and is prone to earthquakes and volcanic eruptions. It has also been hit by many hurricanes.

Human activities have threatened Central America's environment, too. Rain forest has been cut down, destroying the habitats of many animals and weakening the ability of the soil to support plants and trees.

In Costa Rica, rain forest is being cut down or burnt to clear land for farming.

El Niño probably has the greatest affect on Central America's ecosystem. The region needs to receive a certain quantity of water each month to maintain its crops and supply water to its people.

During El Niño, which occurs about every two to seven years, Central America receives little or no rain at all for several months. Other regions are also affected by El Niño. The Philippines, Australia, and Indonesia experienced drought during the 1997–1998 El Niño. At the same time, floods occurred in Peru and Ecuador, two countries in South America.

The El Niño of 1997–1998 brought heavy rain to Peru.

El Niño and Ocean Currents

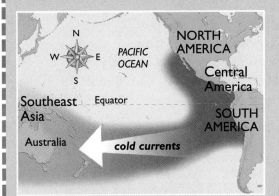

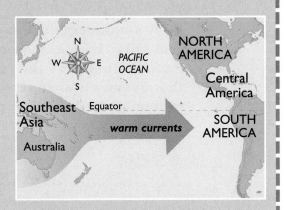

Normal conditions
Most of the time, westerly winds produce ocean currents that carry cool surface waters away from South America toward Australia. This effect brings heavy rainfall to Southeast Asia while cold ocean water rises up along the coast of South America.

El Niño conditions
During El Niño, the westerly winds die down and change direction. Surface currents are reversed. They now carry warm ocean water in an easterly direction across the Pacific Ocean. This change has a dramatic effect on rainfall patterns worldwide.

An Unexpected El Niño

In May 1997, the waters in the Pacific Ocean had already warmed up by 3.6 degrees Fahrenheit in places. Also, storm systems normally found over Indonesia were moving east. Both of these changes were significant clues for meteorologists— a new El Niño was beginning.

In most cases, meteorologists are able to predict El Niño up to a year in advance. However, the scientists didn't realize the 1997 El Niño was under way until six months before the warm water arrived off the coast of South America.

Meteorologists study data about Earth's atmosphere to learn about the weather.

David Parker, an El Niño tracker at England's Meteorological Office, predicted that the 1997 El Niño would have devastating effects. He was correct. This is what he said:

❚❚ The consequences [of El Niño] will probably be felt worldwide over the coming year.... So far, 1997 is already the second warmest year ever, so we could see a new record. ❚❚

Studying El Niño

This satellite photograph shows the warm El Niño current in the Pacific in June 1997. Meteorologists use images like this to help them understand El Niño. Although they know when an El Niño weather pattern is starting to happen, they still do not know why the ocean currents change direction.

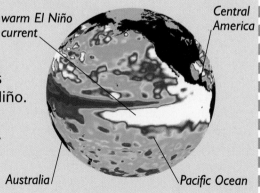

warm El Niño current

Central America

Australia

Pacific Ocean

Devastation

For many months at the end of 1997 and the beginning of 1998, much of Central America was devastated by drought. Crops withered under the hot, dry conditions and the intense heat caused roads to buckle. Rivers and lakes dried up, and the water levels in reservoirs steadily dropped. Some people died from starvation during the drought, and many died from the heat.

Both rural and urban areas were affected. Farmers watched their crops fail, and together with the city dwellers, they suffered food and water shortages.

What Is a Drought?

A drought is an extended shortage of rainfall that is unusual for an area. It is considered to be a temporary condition, even though it can last for months, or even years. Regions that have very low yearly rainfall are considered to be arid, or dry.

A farmer in Honduras surveys his withered maize crop.

The dry weather shriveled trees and other plants, creating conditions perfect for wildfires. As forests burned, animal habitats were destroyed. Many people who worked gathering and selling forest products lost their jobs. Smoke from fires made breathing difficult for people and animals. For months, the skies were polluted by a gray haze of smoke that caused health problems and poor visibility.

Coping With the Disaster

Most countries in Central America were not prepared for the devastating effects of the drought. As harvests failed, people began to starve. Some countries were helped by international aid agencies. Emergency food supplies were shipped to the worst areas. The longer the drought continued, however, the more severe the disaster became.

In Guatemala and other countries in Central America, emergency food supplies were handed out.

In some countries in Central America, including Costa Rica, cattle were herded away from the driest areas.

Other countries, such as Costa Rica, did not request international help. Costa Rica's government limited the effects of the disaster by acting immediately, at the beginning of the drought. First, it declared a "state of emergency," which gave the government more power to control resources, such as water and transportation. The government rationed water, limiting the amount that people could use, so that no water was wasted. They built wells around the country to gain access to more underground water.

The government also organized a national fire-prevention campaign. Throughout the crisis, the government kept Costa Ricans informed about El Niño and its effects.

Central America Today

Costa Rica's programs worked. By May 1998, the country had survived the crisis. They had created a plan to ensure that people would have food and water throughout the drought and to limit damage to livestock and crops. They would know what to do when El Niño and drought returned.

In recent years, drought has returned to Central America frequently, and each time, emergency aid programs have been put in place. However, in a region that is constantly battered by hurricanes, floods, earthquakes, and drought, long-term planning is needed to help the people and their land survive. Costa Rica's handling of the 1997–1998 drought serves as a model to other countries in Central America facing natural disaster.

The beaches of Costa Rica attract tourism, bringing much-needed money into the country.

Handling Natural Disasters

Cyclone Tracy, the Huang He flood, and the drought in Central America all caused major changes in population centers. Cyclone Tracy caused the evacuation of three-quarters of Darwin's population. The 1933 flood in China caused the temporary relocation of millions of citizens. Central America's drought in 1997–1998 forced many people to move to areas with more water.

Natural disasters affect huge groups of people, directly or indirectly. They can bring death, famine, disease, and homelessness, and can destroy landscapes, wiping out crops and cattle.

Because the consequences of natural disasters can be so terrible, it is important to learn how to handle them. In this final section, you can read how international aid organizations provide support to areas hit by disaster. You can also learn how meteorologists and other scientists work toward a greater understanding of Earth and its weather systems.

Other Floods, Droughts, and Tropical Cyclones

The South Asian floods of 2007 affected more than 4 million people, including these Bangladeshis.

For seven years in the 1930s, the United States suffered a severe drought known as the Dust Bowl. It destroyed huge areas of farmland.

In February 2000, heavy rain in southern Africa caused terrible floods in Mozambique. More than 1 million people had to leave their homes.

International Aid Organizations

International disaster-relief agencies help people all over the world who have been affected by severe storms, floods, and drought. For example, the Red Cross and the Red Crescent provide emergency aid when disaster strikes. They supply food, water, clothing, and medicine. They also provide shelter, often tents, for those who have been left homeless.

One of the main roles of relief agencies is to offer comfort and emotional support to people who have been traumatized by natural disaster. Like many relief organizations, the Red Cross and the Red Crescent also set up long-term programs. Volunteers spend months, or even years, in countries in need of their help. They provide equipment and advice that local people can use to help themselves after the aid organizations have left.

A Red Crescent volunteer gives a bag of relief goods to a young victim of flooding in Bangladesh.

A Red Cross worker in Honduras rescues a girl after the overflowing of the Ulua River.

Understanding Earth

Meteorologists and other scientists carefully study tropical storms, floods, droughts, and other natural disasters to learn as much as they can about our planet. They examine data and photographs provided by satellites, searching for patterns in weather systems and changes to Earth's climate. They use special equipment to monitor changes that could indicate that a disaster is about to occur.

The information that these scientists gather is invaluable to people who live in disaster-prone areas. They hope that scientists will be able to predict where, when, and how severe a cyclone or flood will be. With detailed warnings, people can make preparations to try to limit the devastating consequences of natural disasters.

Climate Change

Climate change is a change in Earth's long-term weather patterns. Presently, Earth is experiencing a warming trend. When fossil fuels—coal, oil, and gas—are burned, carbon dioxide gas is released into the atmosphere. Carbon dioxide traps heat and holds it near Earth's surface. In recent years, this "global warming" has caused the ice caps at the poles to begin to melt. The melting of polar ice may result in raised sea levels and a change in ocean currents and rainfall patterns.

Scientists predict that due to global warming, El Niño will be more frequent, resulting in more severe weather conditions. Cutting down on the use of fossil fuels and avoiding pollution of the atmosphere will help to prevent global warming.

Understanding our planet, Earth, can help predict and prevent natural disasters.

Index

Bangladesh 29, 30
Central America 5, 21–28, 29
Chang Jiang (Yangtze River)
   13, 20
China 5, 13–20, 29
climate change 31
Collins, Bob 7, 8, 9, 10
Costa Rica 5, 21, 22, 27, 28
Cyclone Tracy 5, 6–12, 29
cyclones 5, 6, 7, 8, 12, 29, 31
Darwin, Australia 5, 6–12, 29
dike 15, 16, 17, 18
drought 5, 20, 21–28, 29, 30, 31
Earth 29, 31
El Niño 21, 23, 24, 27, 28, 31
eye of a cyclone 8
floods 5, 13–20, 21, 22, 23,
   28, 29, 30, 31
forest fires 21, 26
Guatemala 21, 27
Honduras 21, 22, 25, 30
Huang He (Yellow River) 5,
   13–20

Hurricane Mitch 22, 30
hurricanes 7, 22, 28
international aid agencies
   27, 29, 30
kaoliang 17
Lawrie, Dawn 11
meteorologists 24, 29, 31
Mozambique 29
Nicaragua 21, 22
ocean currents 23, 24, 31
Paiyuan, Du 20
Parker, David 24
Peru 23
Red Crescent 30
Red Cross 30
silt 13, 14, 15, 16, 20
starvation 5, 19, 25, 27
tornadoes 4
typhoons 7
United States 29
Wesley-Smith, Rob 8, 10
winds 4, 5, 6, 7, 8, 12,
   21, 23